The Magic of the Heart

Swami
Chidvilasananda

The Magic of the Heart

Reflections
on Divine Love

A SIDDHA YOGA PUBLICATION
PUBLISHED BY SYDA FOUNDATION

*ll of God's treasures and miracles
are hidden within the heart
of everything that lives.*

Swami Chidvilasananda

Front cover: *In the scriptures of the Indian tradition, the Supreme Heart in an individual is seated in the crown of the head, the* sahasrara. *Here, in the effulgent thousand-petaled lotus, scintillates the Blue Pearl, the seed of the universe. This fascinating blue light, the divine light of Consciousness, is the form of God, the form of the Self that lives within us.*

Published by SYDA Foundation
371 Brickman Rd., P.O. Box 600, South Fallsburg, NY 12779, USA

Acknowledgments
Many, many thanks to all the lovers of Love who offered their suggestions for this volume. And especially great appreciation to Sarah Scott for her editorial assistance. The designer Cheryl Crawford, the typesetter Stéphane Dehais, and the production team of Osnat Shurer, Sushila Traverse, and Valerie Sensabaugh offered their always creative services. The reflections in The Magic of the Heart *are selected from the spoken and written words of Gurumayi Chidvilasananda, and we are deeply grateful to all those who have, over the years, faithfully recorded the Master's wisdom.*

Kshama Jane Ferrar

First published 1996
Printed in the United States of America
00 99 98 97 96   5 4 3 2 1

Library of Congress Catalog Card Number: 96:70628
ISBN 0-911307-43-5

Contents

Swami Chidvilasananda and the Siddha Yoga Tradition

Swami Chidvilasananda is a Siddha Master, an enlightened teacher who initiates and guides seekers on the spiritual path. Heir to an ancient lineage of Siddhas, Gurumayi Chidvilasananda received the power to transmit spiritual energy from her Master, Swami Muktananda. At the instruction of his Guru, the revered saint Bhagawan Nityananda, Swami Muktananda brought the mysterious and previously secret experience of *shaktipat* initiation to the West during the last twelve years of his life.

Since her Guru's passing in 1982, Gurumayi has continued in this tradition, freely bestowing the spiritual awakening of *shaktipat,* and guiding the development of seekers throughout the world. Wherever Gurumayi goes, whatever she says, whatever actions she performs, she conveys the Siddhas' message of love: love for God, love for the inner Self, love for the natural universe, love for all beings. "It should not be a surprise that we want to spread God's light in this world," she says. "That is why we are born. The purpose of human birth is to live the life of God, a life filled with love."

On the path of Siddha Yoga, the attainment of this constant love comes through the exquisite interplay between the Master's grace and the seeker's effort. Eventually the seeker, lifted out of his or her limited identity, soars into a state of freedom, filled with compassion and God's unconditional love. This is the promise and the blessing of the Siddha Yoga Masters.

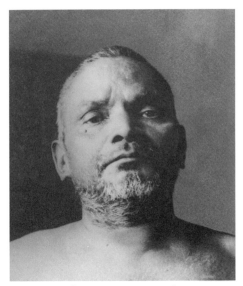

Bhagawan Nityananda

Swami Muktananda

Introduction

Once, when I was quite young, kneeling at the back of a darkened chapel, I found myself suddenly thinking that I could, if I wanted, choose sainthood for my life's work. The idea stunned me with its clarity and simplicity, and I turned it over several times. But almost as quickly as the thought had come to me, I backed away from it. Images of arduous penances crowded my mind, of hair shirts, self-imposed suffering, joyless discipline. "Too hard," I told myself, "and, what's more, sainthood is no way to make a living." As I was refusing sainthood in that moment, I was also suppressing something as essential to myself as breathing — a love of the sacred to which I had been intuitively drawn from early childhood on. Despite my mind's cautionary interference, my heart turned me again and again to the mystery of religious ritual, the delicately strong tracery of the Gothic cathedrals of Europe, the other-worldly beauty of Christian mystical writings, and the poetry of the Buddhist saints.

For many years after that moment in the chapel, I studied and then taught the medieval poetry of spiritual vision; yet always I kept my heart carefully in check. From time to time, usually in prayer, I would find myself transported unexpectedly into a transcendent state of tranquility, joy, or gratitude. In such moments, I knew that I had been moved by God's love, by an experience of divine presence of the kind the great mystic, Saint Teresa of Avila, called a "delectable tempest." Fleetingly I would experience a space within myself — not physical but spiritual — where I knew absolute peace, perfect contentment. But I treated such glimpses of peace and joy as coming from outside myself, not mine to preserve, cultivate, or own. I was simply afraid to turn from the safety of books (and ego and mind) to confront the heart's deepest yearning. That would be to risk too much. It might even carry me over the threshold of a realm I preferred to leave to the poets and cathedral builders and saints — the realm of divine love.

I might well have lived out my entire life clinging to part-time, partial love, my mind always pulling me away from my heart. Yet, when I least expected and most needed it, an amazing grace settled me on a new (but also ancient) path, bringing with it a life-transforming grasp of what it means to love. Through the spiritual traditions and practices of India that the Siddha Master Swami Muktananda was interpreting and introducing to seekers in the West, I began to move — slowly and tentatively — from an intellectual grasp of the heart's power to the direct experience of it. It was through the teachings of Siddha Yoga, first from Baba Muktananda two decades ago, then from Gurumayi Chidvilasananda, that I came to understand how essential it is to let the mind "ripen" and "mature," as Gurumayi puts it so beautifully, "in the lotus of the heart." Even more, I learned that I myself could aspire, through faith and courage, to "enter God's heart."

Page after page, Gurumayi's words in *The Magic of the Heart* point us directly, unrelentingly, to that inner space of the spiritual heart (quite other than the physical heart) where the divine Light steadily burns. With a simplicity born of deep wisdom and grace, Gurumayi penetrates to the core of a great mystery — the mystery of the heart in love with God. This love requires experience beyond words for its full understanding, and it is obvious from every word Gurumayi speaks that she not only lives the experience but yearns to draw everyone to it. Taken together, the lessons of her book teach the importance — the necessity — of giving up our part-time attention to love (or loves, as if they were all separate from each other) in order to become *full-time* lovers. Saints know that to love, and to be *continually* in love with, God is the secret of perfect contentment. As a Siddha herself, Gurumayi reminds us over and over in the pages of this exquisite book that we are all, here and now, saints-in-the-making, all capable of following the spiritual path to the Light of Lights within us.

How, though, do we become saints? Must we leave spouses, family, friends, jobs, to retreat to a cave in the wilderness, a desert, a monastery? Not at all. Grace will draw us to divine love, if only we give our heart's space to it. And grace will bless us into sainthood. This key teaching of Gurumayi is one that has been repeated through the ages by all of the great saints and religious traditions. "*You* arouse us," Saint Augustine wrote over fifteen centuries ago, addressing God, "to take joy in praising You, for You have made us for Yourself, and our heart is restless until it rests in You." So too Lord Krishna tells Arjuna in the *Bhagavad Gita*, "Those who set their hearts on Me and, ever in love, worship Me, and who have unshakable faith, these I hold as the best yogis." And Gurumayi tells us confidently, "When you reside in God's love completely, it is His strength you attain."

The secret of finding the rest Augustine speaks of, the perfection Krishna preaches to Arjuna, the divine strength

Gurumayi promises, lies in the totality and constancy of our commitment to love. Those who are *ever* in love, who reside *completely* in God's love, will find the stable joy and peace promised to saints, both in the world and beyond it.

The twin pillars supporting the heart's growth toward the full-time love of sainthood are faith and devotion. As the great sixth-century monk Saint Benedict declared in his *Rule for Monks*, "We are about to open a school for God's service.... As our lives and faith progress, the heart expands and with the sweetness of love we move down the paths of God's commandments." The process of expanding the heart begins with a deep belief that transformation is possible; progress depends on steady devotion, which, in the spiritual tradition of India, is called *parabhakti*. Gently but firmly, Gurumayi's lessons in *The Magic of the Heart* outline the practical steps needed to stir devotion and cultivate the love of God. The love she teaches is, she says, "something you learn again and again," something that requires attention, effort, and humility.

What are the devotional practices necessary to become a full-time lover, a saint-in-the-making? Regular chanting, repetition of the mantra, meditation, silent contemplation all help to quiet the restless mind, thereby allowing "a seeker to drink the nectarean light of the heart." These practices demand discipline. To prepare the terrain of the spiritual heart to receive divine love requires the quieting of all those impulses the mind has to wander off into the labyrinths of thought. But the reward the Guru promises for devotional effort far exceeds the austerity of the discipline. As Gurumayi says, "Your heart will be so light that you will become everything you ever wanted to be." When the heart opens in this way, you may well find the outward circumstances of your life changing, sometimes dramatically. More importantly, you will notice astonishing changes in your way of seeing and responding to all that happens to you, all that you do.

This is the magic worked within and by the heart as you invite and accept the grace to love God completely. "A subtle alchemy takes place," Gurumayi assures us, "when God's love arises in your heart. It brings about the sweetest changes in your life; it creates a beautiful change within yourself." The Magic of the Heart charts the way to achieve this alchemy. To absorb its teachings and draw them into your heart will give you the strength to move forward right now, in this moment, on the path of love, the way to sainthood.

Professor Barbara Nolan

Barbara Nolan is Robert C. Taylor Professor of English and Vice Provost at the University of Virginia. A former Guggenheim fellow and Fullbright scholar, she is the author of two important books on medieval literature, The Gothic Visionary Perspective *and* Chaucer and the Tradition of the Roman Antique.

The Heart, the Chamber of Light

he eternal, pure, and blissful Self
abides in the heart,
the chamber of light.

*hen the heart opens,
the path to liberation lies before you.*

he heart has always been represented
as the source of human kindness,
the wellspring of warmth and tender care.
It is the cup that holds
the nectar of compassion.

The heart is also
the most sacred place of worship
from which devotion flows like honey.
All virtues make their home
in the infinite space
shining in the depths of the heart.

ithin the heart there is a beautiful flame
the size of your thumb.
It is full of knowledge, full of love.
This divine flame gives luster to your body.
It gives power to your mind.

This divine flame in the cave of your heart
allows you to love others.

*he cave of the heart shines brilliantly:
it blazes with a self-born light.*

*Without either sun or moon,
the cave of the heart
is lit by itself.*

If a ferris wheel is broken,
you can change the seats a hundred times
and paint it every color under the sun,
but only when you fix the hub
will the wheel revolve.

To put it very simply,
to immerse yourself in the heart
is to make yourself new,
not just once, but over and over again.

Come to rest in the heart.
That is what enables you to experience
the glory of life.

he heart is supreme Consciousness.
It is the power of bliss,
the power of freedom.
Undying and unborn,
it is the sum total
of both existence and nonexistence.

To savor this bliss and freedom,
you must make a steady effort
to enter the silence of the heart.

he silence of the heart is luminous
and completely peaceful.
From this sacred place
it flows into the rest of your life.

*llow your mind to turn within
again and again
to experience its own inner silence.
When you do, divine light blazes forth,
which you perceive as the light
of your own heart.*

ou cannot enter the heart from outside.
You must emerge from the lake of the heart.
It is from within that the experience springs forth.

nly after experiencing That,
the innermost Self dwelling
in the cave of the heart,
do you know the fullness of your life.

Then everything you do becomes worship.
Everything you say becomes mantra.
All your activities are permeated with shakti,
the great spiritual energy.

ust as you insert a thread
into the eye of a needle
to make it ready to sew,
similarly, you pass your life
through the eye of the heart
so that you may become fit
to serve God with the knowledge of Him.

eep your heart sweet.
It will show on your face,
it will sound in your words,
it will shine in all your actions.

*I*f you truly follow the heart's intentions,
nothing can deter you.
Everything that happens
will turn out to your own advantage.
You will extract nectar
from the essence of every flower.

he heart can become fully satisfied
when it is drenched in God's love.
That happens when you experience
true aloneness,
being alone with God.
Not loneliness, but true aloneness.

hen you come to know the heart
as the supreme abode of the Lord,
you are set free from the grip
of worldly attractions.
Then truly you are able to say
you have been given a radiant life,
a blessed life.

ive yourself to your own heart
and you will feel God's love;
you will feel that you are loved by God.

God is without visible form,
yet in the heart, God is revealed.

*s you experience closeness with the Lord,
your heart becomes as great as His.*

he experience of becoming one
with the supreme Lord in your own heart
is true liberation.

An open and pure heart
is where this union takes place.

Liberation is nothing more,
nothing less,
than becoming established
in the constant experience
of an open, unfettered heart.

et your heart
become so saturated with love
that you are able to ride the waves of change
with equipoise
and find new meaning
in everything that happens.

The Heart, the Chamber of Light

t is love that has brought us together
on this magnificent planet called earth.
We are blessed with stars and a moon,
high-peaked mountains,
roaring oceans, shining crystals,
fresh food and bread:
so many blessings, so much grace.

The most sublime blessing of all
is the pure heart.

hen a drop of love
from a pure heart falls
on dry ground, the most exquisite
flower of new life emerges.

To know ecstasy,
to know the beauty
and the love of God,
you must have a humble heart.

Love itself is so pure
that only a pure heart
can sustain the experience of it.

o experience the purity,
the greatness, of the heart
is the blessing of all Siddhas.

The Heart, the Chamber of Light

*nce you experience God
in the cave of your own heart,
you begin to perceive His energy
dancing through every cell of your body,
permeating your life.
And you wonder in amazement,
"How could such glory
have remained hidden from me for so long?"*

It is for this reason we meditate.

God's Love in Its Fullness

he scriptures say God's love is the perfect love.
It is the fullest love; it never wanes.
Free from any ebb and flow,
it neither increases nor decreases.
It is as present in darkness as it is in light,
as present in the nether worlds
as in the heavens.
There is no place, no time
where God's love is not manifest.
It is satchidananda,
Truth, Consciousness, and Bliss.
It exists in all places, in all things,
and at all times in the same measure.
Its perfection, its fullness
can never be erased.

ome people actually treat divine love
like a birthday cake.
They think the more people who come to the party,
the smaller each person's piece of cake will be.
There is always a fear of running out of cake
or of receiving only a few crumbs.

God's love for you
is not like a piece of birthday cake.
God's love for you is perfect,
and in its perfection, it is vast and unending.
This is the unparalleled glory of God's love.
Its inexhaustible wellspring never runs dry.

o matter how many people
participate in receiving God's love,
there is always more.

No matter how many thousands of people
bathe in the ocean, there is still
plenty of water for each of them.
No matter how many people
watch the rising sun,
its grandeur never pales.
No matter how many devotees
have mystical experiences,
the intensity of that divine energy,
the source of all experiences,
never fades.
It is as strong as ever, as giving as ever.

*hatever you receive
from God's love in its fullness,
that fullness remains
forever full.*

*I*n His giving,
 there is no holding back.
In His *caring,*
 there is no apathy.
In His *loving,*
 there is no measure.
In His *embrace,*
 there is no expectation.

In His *unending song,*
 there is the gift of life.

*f you want to experience God's love
in its fullness,
offer yourself at His feet.*

*I*n the Bhagavad Gita, *the Lord says:*
"I am the love that is never contrary to dharma."
What does the Lord mean?
This love is the highest energy
that is transmuted into dharmic actions.
This love knows itself.

It is the power of intuition,
the power of resolution,
the power of patience.
It is the power behind forgiveness,
compassion, and service.
It is both soft and hard,
small and great,
visible and invisible, all at once.
It is free from lust and passion.

This love is pure nectar.
It knows no fear.
It is the all-perceiving eye
that is ever gracious.

*t is true that God's love in its fullness
permeates the entire universe.
However, it is only when you follow dharma,
the immortal law of the Lord,
that you come to appreciate deeply
the presence of divine Love.*

s you go about your daily duties,
learn to perceive everything that happens
as a message from God's house.
Then every activity, every moment of your life,
will scintillate with Love.

*o experience God's love in its fullness,
you need to have a subtle eye:
the subtle eye you receive through grace.*

od's attributes are your attributes.
God's virtues are your virtues.
God's love is your love.

*hen you reside in God's love completely,
it is His strength you attain.*

God's Love in Its Fullness

hat is the final outcome
of experiencing God's love in its fullness?

He makes you like Himself;
He gives Himself totally to you.
You have the profound experience,
"I am That."

hen you experience God's love in its fullness,
you have complete trust
that whatever happens,
happens for the best.

od's tender love
makes you into a person
completely undaunted
by the extremes of life.

od's love is so flawlessly beautiful
that it holds your heart
in deep silence.

God's Love in Its Fullness

*A*t times
you may feel completely engulfed
by unconditional love.
And yet, you may feel
you still need to experience
more of this love.

That is called longing.
It is a beneficial desire.

Though you may feel at times
your heart is going to burst
because it is aching
with such strong love,
don't pray to lower the heat,
to lessen the intensity;
just go through it.

Follow the beckoning of God's heart.

earning is very important on the spiritual path.
If you yearn to know something,
you will definitely get the answer.
If you yearn to love God,
without a doubt you will receive this love.

very tear you shed in the love of God
is worth a hundred practices;
every wakeful night in the love of God
is worth a hundred visions.

s the reality of God's love
makes its presence known in your life,
you begin to perceive that God's love
is impartial.
God's love is unconditional.
It is completely available
to anyone who is willing to be open
and willing to experience it.

o melt into His enthusiasm
and be the song in His heart,
to melt into His eyes
and be the vision of His sight,
to surrender into His hands
and be His servant,
to merge into His love
and be His Beloved
is to embrace His enthusiasm
and sing His glory
through all of time and eternity.

henever God's love is discussed,
whenever God's love is experienced,
all the Siddhas and great beings,
all the saints,
all the gods and goddesses,
all the yogis and renunciants,
and all the beings who adore God
come and participate in the gathering.

*Y*ou and Love Are One and the Same

*ehold the interior of your soul,
the inner chambers of the heart.
The Lord reveals Himself there
every second of the day.*

To have the vision of God,
you must believe
that God dwells within you
as you,
that the divine Presence
is seated in your heart.
This must become your conviction.

Then, when He reveals Himself to you
in the form of love,
you will be able to honor the experience.

od's love is divine
because it gives of itself.
When the sun rises,
we revel in its glory.
When waterfalls cascade
and meet the earth below,
we marvel at their splendor.
When we witness the mountains,
standing still in all their majesty,
they take our breath away.
All these things
give fully of themselves,
revealing God's love.

In the same way,
love arises in our hearts
with all its brilliance
and gives of itself,
and therefore it is called divine love.

subtle alchemy takes place
when God's love
arises in your heart.
It brings about
the sweetest changes in your life;
it creates a beautiful change
within yourself.

As tender as this love may be,
it is full of God's power.
It strengthens the heart,
it purifies the mind.
This love fortifies your faith in God.

od pulls your heart to Him
and makes it His own.
When this happens,
you feel so close to God
there is no longer any separation,
and your heart is able to drink the nectar
of its own divinity.

ou are the bearer
of the kingdom of love.

Doesn't it make you feel
more humble than humility itself
to realize God's immense compassion
and unconditional love?

ompletion, union with God,
comes about when you
give yourself to God completely,
deep in your heart.

It is not an external posture;
it is a mysterious internal happening.

*I*n the Maitri Upanishad,
one of the ancient scriptures of India,
the sage says:

> The sun of Consciousness
> ever shines resplendent
> in the space of the heart.

When you perceive the beauty
that lies within you,
Consciousness blazing like the sun,
you become aware of who you really are.

he freedom that you experience
in the presence of the great Light
makes you soar without wings.
Your heart becomes unimaginably buoyant,
so full of love, that an inner door opens.
Through this doorway
you realize the glory of God in your own heart.

he flame of love
is not different from you;
it is you.

It isn't that love is there
and you are here.
You and love
are one and the same.

Love is self-born.
You don't have to wait
for someone to give you love.

For the gift of love to grow,
you pour love into love.
To keep love growing,
to keep love burning high,
you add love to love.
No other ingredient,
no other substance is required.

*ivine love cannot change itself
into anything other
than what it is.*

o matter how we judge the course of love,
it is not judged by our judgments.
This is why the sages tell us:
become love.
There is no point in wondering
how love should be,
how love can be.
Become love as it is.

upreme love
in its fullness
is free;
it is ecstatic within itself.

hen there is love
and nothing but love,
what else can there be
but total absorption
in the supreme Self?

You give love, you take love;
you sit in love, you stand in love;
you sleep in love, you wake up in love:
all around you, nothing but love.

hen you are totally saturated with love, nothing matters but love.

ecome aware of God's power
within yourself.
Understand that saintliness
is not a gift that God confers
on only a chosen few.
It is a treasure
that God has placed
within every child of His.

elcoming the wind, the sunshine,
the days, the nights,
every moment, every person,
every object, every task,
with the joy in your own heart
and also knowing,
beyond a shadow of a doubt,
that joy is what you will receive from them:
in this way you create
a palace of joy to live in.

*I*n this human birth,
you can make a daring attempt
to attain perfect joy, perfect love.
The scriptures and the great beings say
with great authority and great conviction,
"It is possible."
Yes.
You can experience
perfect joy, perfect love,
in this very human body.

ever doubt the experiences of your own heart.
Never put the experiences in an attic
nor bury them in the depths of the ocean.
Let your experiences shine forth;
let the world see
that you have a great diamond
you carry everywhere:
God's love.

sn't it great good fortune
to breathe God's love,
which is softer than silk
and more powerful than a thunderbolt?
Don't you feel blessed
that God has beckoned you
to dwell in His house, in this body
made of immortal love?
Don't you feel honored
to carry the supreme abode
within your own being?

Devotion: the Exquisite Virtue

The purest love of all,
the feeling called devotion,
is even more brilliant
than the millions of stars
scattered across the soft night sky.

O f all the virtues,
devotion
is the most exquisite.

hatever your lifestyle may have been,
understand one thing:
the moment you're affected by love,
the moment devotion has risen within you,
that is the path you must follow.

Love is the right decision.

oving God
liberates you
from the noose of this world.

*evotion
cures the karmas
of many births.*

n true devotion you accept God's supremacy.
This is what opens your heart to His love,
to the magnificence of the five elements —
water, earth, fire, air, and ether —
to the whimsy of a speck of dust,
to the tiny eyes of an ant,
to the infinitely varied
sounds, lights, and colors of the universe.

Who but the supreme Lord
could fashion such a glorious creation?

There are many kinds of devotion,
many stages in devotion,
and the highest stage
is called parabhakti.
This is the supreme devotion
in which the Lord and the devotee
merge into each other completely,
and the devotee knows nothing else
but the Lord.

hen you are freed from the grasp of doership,
even if it is just for a moment,
immediately parabhakti, supreme devotion,
takes its place.

hen you are not honored,
when you are not praised,
when you are not given any credit
for everything you do in your life,
and you still feel love for humanity,
you still feel love for God —
then know that true love has arisen in your heart.

ake devotion your goal
and install it where you usually keep
all thoughts of reward.
If you do, you will experience
the eternal spring of devotion
flowing through every nadi,
every subtle channel in your body.
You will experience devotion
flowing through all of your life.

*anting to be submerged
in the profound silence
of your true nature
is devotion.
When you want to experience
the inner silence,
understand you are in love;
you are in love with God.*

*You feel love for God,
and that feeling itself is God.*

Devotion: the Exquisite Virtue

*hen the heart overflows with humility,
then you are able to experience
pure devotion to God.*

*It is unconditional love for God
that allows you to experience God's company
and God's support.*

*evotion gives you the tremendous
courage you need to keep walking
on the path.*

*When it is necessary to make
a great leap forward,
devotion gives you wings.*

ou must not waver in your steadfastness
just because something goes awry.
Have one-pointed devotion.
Only then do you have the strength
to bear the immensity of God's love for you.
Otherwise, with every little discomfort,
you are quick to forget God's love.

To attain parabhakti,
supreme love,
you must be fearless.

Relationships may come and go,
your understanding may come and go,
prosperity and good times may come and go.
But if your devotion is steady,
again and again it will bring about
all that you need to nourish yourself.

magine raindrops falling on parched earth.
Can you picture how the ground softens and yields?
In the same way, drops of devotion
bring out the best in the heart.

*ven one drop of devotion
inspires amazing experiences
of the supreme Self.*

hakti, devotion,
is a pure expression
of the inner Self.
There is no ulterior motive.
It just is.

This perfect simplicity
of being and effort
is a reflection of the love
abounding in the created world.

Devotion: the Exquisite Virtue

hen bhakti *arises,*
its possibilities
and its sweetness
are unlimited.
How can this be?

Because bhakti
is free from attachment.
As long as there is attachment,
there are conditions.

Pure devotion
is free from attachment.

Even an iota of devotion
moves the Lord
to come to the aid of His devotee.
And to one whose heart is full of devotion,
the Lord wants to give everything.

*llow your devotion to be so strong
that God cannot hide His face from you.*

hen God is loved,
He becomes totally yours.

*t is devotion that makes
the invisible visible
and the unknown known.*

hen you pray to God
you ask for so many things.
Sooner or later
they will be granted.
Still, what good are material objects,
or even liberation,
without devotion?

If the heart is not moist
singing songs of love,
longing for love
even while being merged in love,
what good is this heart?

*ever undervalue
the power of devotion
to change your experience of the world.*

*I*ntense devotion for God
draws grace.
And this grace manifests
in the form of shaktipat.

t every stage of spiritual life,
devotion is crucial:
first to attract grace;
then to hold grace
and deepen your awareness of its presence;
and finally to guide you
to union with the Absolute,
the source of grace.

ove for God doesn't come easily.
It is the fruit of many many merits.
So if you have love for God in your heart,
know that you have already received
infinite blessings.

The Love of Great Beings

*Out of their love for the people of this earth,
the great beings
take form and live among us.*

hatever desire
a great being may have
is very pure.
It is always aimed toward
the happiness of others,
the upliftment of humanity.
Nothing he does is intended for his own welfare;
everything he does is for the good of all.

he lovers of God
have always found their way to Him
through their Master's compassion.

t doesn't matter
who you are,
what you are,
the compassion of a great saint
will enter your heart,
and your heart will be transformed.

The Love of Great Beings

*B*aba Muktananda attained
parabhakti, *supreme devotion,*
through his intense love and surrender
to his own Master,
Bhagawan Nityananda,
whose grace is never-ending.

It was Baba's experience
that without the intervention of grace,
life is a long dull sleep.

hen you come to the Master,
no matter what your original intentions may be,
you leave with a singular longing
to become established in unconditional love.
Whether you ask for it directly or not,
you are given the gift of unconditional love.

great being can give love
without any motive,
because everything about him has been burned
in the fire of Knowledge,
the Knowledge of God.
If anything remains of him, it is only pure love.

he life of a great being
is a blazing fire of God's love.

hen the Guru's shakti enters a disciple's heart,
a great union takes place.
Seers have tried to describe it
by saying it is like a thousand suns
blazing simultaneously across the inner sky.

or a seeker on this path,
the highest goal is the Guru's love
that springs forth in your own heart.

he Guru's love
is full of sweetness,
full of fire.
Allow yourself to be engulfed
by its sweetness.
Allow yourself to be consumed
by its great fire.

*et the sweetness
and the fire
of the Guru's love
reveal the true company that you keep:
the company of God both within and without.*

The Love of Great Beings

aving received the Guru's grace,
the true disciple plunges inside
again and again,
receiving the darshan of God
within his awakened heart.

*ut of the awakened heart
arises a waterfall of experiences.
The only thing a disciple can do
is bathe in the purifying waters
and become one with That.*

*he better you come to know the saints,
the more you will come to trust them.
Develop full faith in their teachings
and in their experiences of God.
They will be an anchor for you.*

he teachings of the scriptures
and the words of great saints
guide us through the darkness of the world.
They are like beacons on the shore
or like the sound of a dear voice calling us home.
They make our spiritual life glow
with deeper understanding
and greater assurance of God's love.

The Love of Great Beings

*T*hrough their words,
the saints pour their own force,
their own shakti, into you
and make you steadfast.
They make your understanding subtle and profound.
You have something to hold on to
during the stormy weather in your life.

here is never a moment when
you are separate from the Guru's love.

In your greatest joys and deepest sorrows,
know that this love shines blissfully.
In your most ecstatic times, in profound miseries,
understand that this love shines brilliantly.
In still moments and moments filled with
tremendous activity, this love shines endlessly.
In your brightest hours and hours filled with darkness,
this love shines compassionately.

Learn to rest your entire being
in the Guru's protection,
in the Guru's love.

he Guru's love is immense.
It is overwhelming.

To contain that love
in this body
is itself the blessing of the Guru's grace.

he Guru's mantra is your total support.
The Guru's teaching is your supreme guide.
The Guru's house is your true abode.
The Guru's love is the breath of your life.

et your entire being shimmer with God's love.
Let your entire being
scintillate with the Guru's love.
Be the carrier of the Guru's love.
And finally, be the Guru's love.

Dissolving the Obstacles

isten!
Today is the auspicious day
to free yourself from the grip of the inner enemies —
desire, anger, greed,
envy, pride, and delusion —
then you can discover the wellspring of enthusiasm
and sing God's glory.

ou don't have to be tricked
by your own ego,
you don't have to be swayed
by your own pride.
Just keep yourself open
to God's will, to God's vision;
allow the love in your heart to overflow.

hen someone asks,
"How can I open my heart?"
the only answer that can be given is,
"When your limited identity dissolves,
you will find your heart is already open."

*ove is a great force that
can remove the tendencies
that build up your ego.*

Don't get confused
between your passion and love,
between your worry and love,
between your familiar ways and love.
Keep your love as pure as possible.

The nature of the mind is very greedy.
The nature of the heart is to become satisfied
with whatever comes its way.
So the marriage
between the mind and the heart
must take place
for you to taste the nectar of tranquility,
the elixir of immortality.

he goodness of your heart is such
that it wants your mind
to have beautiful thoughts.

B y renouncing all concepts,
by allowing the mind to enter new dimensions,
you let love shine forth.

et the mind spend a little time
in the light of the heart,
in the lotus of the heart.
Let the mind rest in this luminous light.
The mind will ripen in the heart
and become mature.
Liberation is possible.

*J*ust as when you put a rock into the ocean,
and slowly, gradually, the rock descends
to the bottom,
in the same way,
let your mind descend into the heart.
It is God's heart.

Behold the interior of God's heart.
What is it made of?
What does it contain?
What message does God's heart have for you?

Allow your mind very gently
to enter God's heart.

roblems in life will always exist,
but through the recognition
of your own heart
a higher awareness comes about,
and you are able to see a greater purpose
in everything that happens.

*A true lover of God
perceives all the pain and challenges of life
as signposts of God's love
along the spiritual path.
He knows that things come up
in order to draw him more deeply
into God's heart.*

ifficulties and challenges
are not there to ruin your life.
They are there to make you strong,
to make you experience the love of God,
the company of God.

nly love can penetrate
all your karmas and resistances
and set your heart on fire
with the awareness of its true nature.

Dissolving the Obstacles

eople often ask,
"How can I experience
the splendor and strength
of the heart?
How can I attain
evenness of mind?"

Continually welcome
God's grace in your life
and allow your pride
to be washed away in devotion.

*ride has no place
in the abode of love.*

*No matter what disguise pride is wearing,
it makes all kinds of demands
in the name of love.*

*nly devotion can conquer
the power of ego.
Devotion carries humility within itself.*

hen you allow devotion
to spring forth, you are freed
from the clutches of moha, delusion.

here is no shortcut.
The only way to release yourself
from the grip of illusion
is to surround yourself
with the love of God,
and in return, capture God's heart,
full of love, full of treasures.

ach time you question God's love for you, do you ever think of doubting your own doubt?

f there is any part of your being
that you have been hiding from God,
let it go.
Let the light of God shine
upon each cell of your being.

Have the firm conviction,
God loves you.

Dissolving the Obstacles

*nce the greatness
of your own heart is realized,
all petty actions fall away.
You don't have to worry
about giving them up;
they will fall away.*

Supporters of Love

hen you chant and meditate,
when you offer seva,
when you contemplate
and perform worship,
you are stepping into the fullness
of God's love.

ne of the most magical things that happens
when you apply yourself to spiritual practices
is that you experience great love
surging within yourself
for no apparent reason.

This love is totally free.
It has no motive.
It is as though this pure love
loves itself.

Very naturally, then, you will be inclined
to let your own goodness shine forth.

henever you say,
"I want to know my own Self,
I want to meditate on my own Self,"
understand that devotion
has taken up residence within you.

The moment you want to become aware
of your own true nature,
you are filled with love.

ithout devotion,
even the spiritual practices
you are most drawn to
can become tedious.

When there is love,
all attainments become accessible.

emember, it is the attitude you adopt
and the love you pour into each practice
that will take you to the highest worship of all,
experiencing the presence of God in everything.

*J*ust as when you kindle a fire
you must create a space to contain it,
in the same way,
you need the tenets of yoga,
you need discipline and understanding,
so that you can hold the experience
of the heart opening.

henever you exercise restraint or self-control,
you create a larger and larger vessel
to contain love,
to experience love.

In this way,
you preserve the energy of love
in your being.

s you walk the spiritual path,
you must keep an eye
on the state of your heart.

How do you do this?
By remaining vigilant.

You need to find out
what goes into the heart
and what comes out of the heart,
who comes into the heart
and who goes out of the heart,
what you store in the heart
and what you reject from the heart,
what your heart likes
and what your heart does not like.

You must be there with your heart,
you must examine its state.

he eye of the heart
is so important in your life.
It can see what is hidden
from the senses.

*S*ometimes people ask,
"Why do I cry when chanting begins?"

When your heart is moved,
you experience the nectar of the heart,
and it flows like tears.
These are not the tears of sadness;
they are tears of the heart's nectar.

ven if you spend a thousand years
reading and studying about God's love,
you barely scratch the surface.
For this reason,
we dive into chanting the name of God.

inging God's glory
not only keeps you away from worry,
it also erases demeaning thoughts
you may hold about yourself.

A singing heart experiences God's beauty.

he knowers of the Truth
repeatedly say: "Sing God's name."

You will be released from
the snares of the world
and regain your freedom.
Your heart will be so light
that you will become
everything you ever wanted to be.

*s you chant
your heart becomes golden
and light radiates from your soul.*

*hanting with love
is the surest way
to reach the heart of God.*

he mantra is the master key
that unlocks the mystery
of the inner kingdom,
revealing the fullness of your own heart.

t is essential on the spiritual path
to embrace the mantra,
to nourish the inner voice,
and to experience the fullness of your own heart.

In this way,
you make yourself whole,
you experience your own wholeness,
and you are able to give your best to life.

he mantra burns away the impurities
in your speech
and makes it luminous.
It injects the nectarean rays of the Truth
into every syllable
and inspires immortal words
that come straight from the heart.

Chanting the mantra
is the culmination of the faculty of speech.

The mantra fills you up with light.
It fills you up with love.
Whenever you are alone,
just repeat the mantra.
Then you will always have good company.

The mantra is the sacred presence within your own being.

henever you find yourself dejected,
bring your mind back
to the splendor of the heart, filled with love,
and listen to the divine sound,
So'ham,
"I am That, I am That,
I am the Truth."

ecause love is so great,
so splendid and adorable,
because love is such a delicious feeling
and contains the power of hope,
because love has such subtle strength,
and is so intoxicating —
like a sudden snowfall
turning everything into a wonderland —
because love has all these qualities,
you want to have them too.

You think love should bestow them all upon you.
You think they should be yours.
You forget you must earn the grace of love.

Remember, love is a spiritual practice,
a sadhana within itself.
Love is an austerity, not a reward.

ove is not something you experience only once,
and then that's it,
there's nothing more to do.

Love is something you learn again and again.

henever you take time
to sit very quietly
and breathe in deep and breathe out long,
you will definitely experience
the power of the heart.

editation is the practice
that helps you keep the company
of your own saintliness.
It is like worshiping the rising sun
within your own heart.

he treasure trove of meditation
brings about supreme rest.
It releases the agitated mind
and bathes it in the fresh energy of the heart.
It loosens the knot of old impressions
and enables a seeker
to drink the nectarean light of the heart.

ive yourself the honor
of experiencing yourself living in God's heart
with great blessings,
with wonderful miracles,
with infinite gratitude and oceans of love.

Meditate while abiding in God's heart.

ust as pilgrims bathe in holy rivers
to experience sanctity
and to become free from sins,
in the same way,
a meditator goes within
and takes a sacred bath
in the profound silence of the heart
to experience divine light.

*he mind that has been anointed
with the balm of silence
allows the light of love
to envelop it.*

f you can succeed in maintaining
the auspicious state of your mind,
then you will find yourself
holding God's glory in your own golden hands.

Wherever you turn, you will be pouring
the delicious nectar of God's light.
Wherever your mind goes,
you will be spreading the mantle of God's love.

Supporters of Love

*T*here must have been a moment in your life
when you wanted nothing,
when you felt entirely content.
Rest in this contentment
and become tranquil.

Contentment opens your heart.

ny time you have
the slightest experience of contentment,
you should know God is present
in your heart.

*A*llow love to stream
through the veins of your body.
When there is love
the body becomes very supple.

Even if you don't feel love,
look at everyone with love,
because love is always there.

It's just that it's not always on the surface.

he truth is that love must be kept alive.
It is not contingent on someone else's effort.
So don't wait for someone else
to make the effort to love you.

For you to experience love,
the effort must be your own;
that is austerity.

*s you become aware of a longing
to serve the highest Truth,
humility begins to illumine your heart.*

*W*hen you do seva with love,
love is what you experience.

henever there is a dry spell
in your sadhana,
in your devotion to God,
understand it's just some old impressions
creeping up.
Keep doing your seva
and don't get buried under their influence.

To maintain the steadiness of the heart
and not get rocked around,
unswerving devotion to the Lord is essential.

Whatever happens,
don't give up your devotion.

*H*aving made the right effort,
you must learn to guard the fruits
of your effort with great care.

It is very important
to protect your own happiness,
to guard your own love.

hen you apply yourself
to spiritual practices,
you experience God's energy so strongly
that you will never again feel
you have to face life alone.
You will feel so loved by God.

Because of this,
your contentment will grow,
your appreciation of life will grow,
and you won't want to waste a single moment.

Love's Mission

eep the company of those beings
who have dedicated themselves
to the many-splendored One.
Find those who have given themselves
to the Almighty.
Such beings truly embody the light of God.
Their very existence is a testimony
to God's love for humanity.
They see with the eyes of God.
They understand the plight of human existence.
The tenderest love that flows from their hearts
removes the most hardened scars
in the soul of all living beings.
Such beings are called saints, great souls.
They have only one goal, one purpose:
to fill this entire universe with love for God.
They have but one vocation:
to sing His glory.

he only thing love knows how to do
is shower goodness
upon everyone it meets.

What can love do
except bring good to others?

t is love that brings us all together
again and again.
It is love that unites us.
It is love that makes time and space collapse.
All barriers come down
because of love.

n the Upanishads it is said:
"All beings are born of love,
all beings live in love,
and ultimately they merge into love."

Love and respect
enable people to overcome
the barriers of religion, tradition,
social custom, and nationality.
Love and respect pave the way,
not only to our immediate goals,
but also to the heart of God.

ove comes from God.
His gift of love
is the bond between us.

The goal of meditation
is parabhakti, *supreme devotion*:
the purest love, the greatest love,
the highest love.
When you have this love,
you feel the same toward everyone.

Even though in the beginning
this love is very one-pointed —
you love God, you love the Guru,
you love your own inner Self —
once the fountain of love
begins to flow in your being,
this love is for everyone.

he glory of parabhakti, supreme love,
cannot really be described in words,
so the wisest and most beneficial thing
you can do is learn to apply
the experience of divine love
to your daily life.

Just as when the sun rises
its rays will fall upon everything,
in the same way,
when God's love arises within you
it will touch everyone else as well.

You will see everything in this world
as an instrument of God's grace.

Many times you think
you don't have time to give love
because you want to find the perfect time,
the perfect gift, the perfect terminology,
the perfect expression, the perfect body,
the perfect everything.
But with God's love, unconditional love,
you don't really have to look
for all these perfect settings.

You can just give a little love at any time.
Don't wait for the perfect environment.
As soon as you feel love, give love.

ou say,
"I'm just a human.
How can I love everyone?"
And the saints say,
"God lives in your heart.
Why can't you love everyone?"

It's a battle that has been going on
between human beings and the saints
for ages!

*ou have so much love,
you can give it to others
at any time.*

How do saints and sages sing God's glory?
Here is their secret:
they are able to perceive and honor
the attributes of God
in all the people they meet.

he saints are able to see goodness
in each person.
And that is what they want people
to recognize in themselves.

Their experience becomes their mission:
to awaken the great power within each person,
so that everyone can come to understand
their own inner glory.

ith the awareness
of God's constant presence
in your life,
you are able to approach
each person and each situation
in a unique way.
Every time it will be different,
every time it will be new,
and every time it will be mysterious.

Love and nothing but love
radiates from your heart
as you meet each person with love,
and each situation
with the greatest understanding.

o recognize God's immense compassion
and accept God's love for all people
is what it means
to keep the company of saints.

*llow the saintliness of others
to shine forth in your own heart.*

ith open hands
the Lord gives and gives and gives.
Simple, constant giving
is the true nature of love.

hen you truly give with love,
there is true abundance.
That is what Baba Muktananda did:
he gave with love,
and therefore
there was always abundance around him.

*W*hen your heart is overflowing,
very naturally
you can see its reflections
glistening everywhere.

he beauty of the universe is perceptible
when the light in your heart
blazes with the awareness of divinity.

Love's Mission

*he greater the feeling you have for this universe,
the more love you feel in your own heart.*

emember: Wherever you are, God is.
We all live in God's heart.

t should not be a surprise
that we want to spread God's light in this world.
That is why we are born.

The purpose of human birth
is to live the life of God,
a life filled with love.

he great teachings portray
the path to God
so beautifully and clearly.
They lay it open before us:
love is the way.

Make a strong effort
to concentrate your mind and heart
on the real reason for living:
to love God, to spread love,
and, ultimately, to merge into love.

Pronunciation Guide

Vowels

Sanskrit vowels are categorized as either long or short. In English transliteration, the long vowels are marked with a bar above the letter and are pronounced twice as long as the short vowels. The vowels *e* and *o* are always pronounced as long vowels.

Short:	Long:
a as in c*u*p	*ā* as in c*a*lm
i as in g*i*ve	*e* as in s*a*ve
u as in f*u*ll	*ī* as in s*ee*n
ṛ as in w*ri*tten	*o* as in ph*o*ne
	ū as in sch*oo*l
	ai as in *ai*sle

Consonants

The main difference between Sanskrit and English pronunciation of consonants is in the aspirated letters. In Sanskrit these are pronounced with a definite *h* sound. The following list shows pronunciation for the Sanskrit consonants found in this book:

bh as in clu*bh*ouse	*ṇ* as in no*n*e
c as in su*ch*	*n* as in s*n*ake
dh as in a*dh*ere	*ś* as in bu*sh*
ḥ is an aspiration	*ṣ* as in *sh*ine
ṃ is a strong nasal *m*	*s* as in *s*upreme

In the text, Sanskrit words appear in simple transliteration. The full transliteration for each Sanskrit term is presented in the glossary in brackets. For a detailed pronunciation guide, see *The Nectar of Chanting*, published by SYDA Foundation.

lossary

Absolute, the

The highest Reality; supreme Consciousness; the pure, untainted, changeless Truth.

Arjuna [*arjuna*]

One of the warrior heroes of the *Mahabharata*, a great disciple of Lord Krishna. It was to Arjuna that the Lord imparted His teachings in the *Bhagavad Gita. See also Bhagavad Gita*, Krishna, *Mahabharata.*

Augustine, Saint

(354-430) A father of the Latin church; author of *Confessions*, one of the world's great spiritual autobiographies. Saint Augustine had a profound influence on later Christian mystics.

Benedict, Saint

(480-547) Italian monk who founded the Benedictine order. His *Rule for Monks*, which emphasized discipline and hard work, became the foundation of Christian monastic life.

Bhagavad Gita [*bhagavadgītā*]

(lit., song of the Lord) One of the world's great spiritual texts and an essential scripture of India; a portion of the *Mahabharata* in which Lord Krishna instructs his disciple Arjuna on the nature of the universe, God, and the supreme Self.

bhakti [*bhakti*]

The path of devotion; a path to union with the Divine based on the continual offering of love and the constant remembrance of the Lord.

Consciousness

The intelligent, supremely independent, divine Energy that creates, pervades, and supports the entire universe.

darshan [*darśana*]

(lit., to have the sight of) A glimpse or vision of a saint; seeing God or an image of God.

dharma [*dharma*]

(lit., what holds together) Essential duty; righteousness; living in accordance with the divine Will. The highest *dharma* is to recognize the Truth in one's own heart.

karma [*karma*]

(lit., action) 1) Any action: physical, verbal, or mental. 2) Destiny that is caused by past actions.

Krishna [*kṛṣṇa*]

The eighth incarnation of Vishnu, the supreme Lord. The spiritual teachings of Lord Krishna are contained in the *Bhagavad Gita*, a portion of the epic *Mahabharata*. See also *Bhagavad Gita, Mahabharata.*

Mahabharata [*mahābhārata*]

An epic poem in Sanskrit that recounts the struggle between two brothers over a disputed kingdom. It is a vast narrative that contains a wealth of Indian secular and religious lore. The *Bhagavad Gita* occurs in the latter portion of the *Mahabharata*. See also *Bhagavad Gita.*

Maitri Upanishad [*maitryupaniṣad*]

One of the principal Upanishads, recounting the teachings of the sage Maitri. See also Upanishad(s).

mantra [*mantra*]

Sacred words or divine sounds invested with the power to protect, purify, and transform the individual who repeats them. *Om Namah Shivaya* is the initiation mantra of the Siddha Yoga lineage. See also *So'ham.*

moha [*moha*]

Delusion that leads to identification with the body, mind, and senses, preventing one from discerning the Truth.

Muktananda, Swami [*muktānanda*]

(*1908-1982; Muktananda, lit., the bliss of freedom*) Swami Chidvilasananda's Guru, often referred to as Baba. This great Siddha brought the powerful and rare initiation known as *shaktipat* to the West at the command of his own Guru, Bhagawan Nityananda. As the inheritor of this lineage of spiritual Masters, Baba Muktananda introduced the path of Siddha Yoga to seekers all over the world, creating what he called a "meditation revolution." He made the scriptures come alive, teaching in words and action, by example and by direct experience.

nadi [*nādī*]

A channel in the subtle body through which the vital force flows.

Om Namah Shivaya [*oṃ namaḥ śivāya*]

(*lit., Om, salutations to Shiva*) The Sanskrit initiation mantra of the Siddha Yoga lineage. *Om* is the primordial sound; *Namah* means to honor; *Shiva* denotes divine Consciousness, the Lord who dwells in every heart. *See also* Mantra.

parabhakti [*parabhakti*]

Supreme love of the Lord, characterized by complete selflessness.

sadhana [*sādhanā*]

1) A spiritual discipline or path. 2) Practices, both physical and mental, on the spiritual path.

satchidananda [*saccidānanda*]

(*lit., absolute Existence, Consciousness, and Bliss*) The three indivisible qualities used to describe the experience of the Absolute.

Self

Divine Consciousness residing in the individual.

seva [*sevā*]

(*lit., service*) Selfless service; work offered to God or to the spiritual Master, performed with love and without concern for its benefits.

shakti [*śakti*]

Spiritual power; the divine cosmic Power that creates and maintains the universe. The dynamic aspect of divine Consciousness.

shaktipat [*śaktipāta*]

(lit., descent of power) The transmission of spiritual energy, *shakti*, from the Guru to the disciple; spiritual awakening by grace.

Siddha(s) [*siddha*]

Perfected yogi; one who is in the state of unity-consciousness or enlightenment; one whose experience of the supreme Self is uninterrupted and whose identification with the ego has been dissolved.

So'ham [*so'ham*]

(lit., That am I) The natural vibration of the Self, which occurs spontaneously with each incoming and outgoing breath. By becoming aware of *So'ham*, a seeker experiences the identity between the individual self and the supreme Self.

Teresa of Avila, Saint

(1515-1582) Spanish Catholic mystic who founded and supervised seventeen convents over a period of twenty years. Saint Teresa wrote about her spiritual experiences and revelations in *The Way of Perfection* and *The Interior Castle*.

Upanishad(s) [*upaniṣad*]

(lit., sitting near steadfastly) The inspired teachings of the ancient sages of India. These scriptures, exceeding one hundred texts, constitute the final and highest knowledge of the Vedas. With immense variety of form and style, all of these texts give the same essential teaching: that the individual soul and God are one.

yoga [*yoga*]

(lit., union) Union with God or the inner Self; a method or practice leading to that state.

Further Reading

SWAMI MUKTANANDA

Play of Consciousness
Bhagawan Nityananda of Ganeshpuri
From the Finite to the Infinite
Where Are You Going?
I Have Become Alive
Mukteshwari
The Perfect Relationship
Reflections of the Self
Secret of the Siddhas
Kundalini

SWAMI CHIDVILASANANDA

The Yoga of Discipline
My Lord Loves a Pure Heart
Inner Treasures
Kindle My Heart
Ashes at My Guru's Feet

CONTEMPLATION BOOKS

Resonate with Stillness
Daily contemplations from the words of
Swami Muktananda, Swami Chidvilasananda

Be Filled with Enthusiasm
Blaze the Trail of Equipoise
Everything Happens for the Best

You may learn more about the teachings and
practices of Siddha Yoga Meditation by contacting:

SYDA Foundation
371 Brickman Rd.
P.O. Box 600
South Fallsburg, NY 12779-0600, USA
Tel: (914) 434-2000

or

Gurudev Siddha Peeth
P.O. Ganeshpuri
PIN 401 206
District Thana
Maharashtra, India

For further information about books in print by Swami Muktananda
and Swami Chidvilasananda, and editions in translation, please contact:

Siddha Yoga Meditation Bookstore
371 Brickman Rd.
P.O. Box 600
South Fallsburg, NY 12779-0600, USA
Tel: (914) 434-2000 ext. 1700